The European Union: The History of the Political and Economic Union of Europe's Nations after World War II

By Charles River Editors

The EU's flag

About Charles River Editors

Charles River Editors provides superior editing and original writing services across the digital publishing industry, with the expertise to create digital content for publishers across a vast range of subject matter. In addition to providing original digital content for third party publishers, we also republish civilization's greatest literary works, bringing them to new generations of readers via ebooks.

Sign up here to receive updates about free books as we publish them, and visit Our Kindle Author Page to browse today's free promotions and our most recently published Kindle titles.

Introduction

Picture of a 1948 congress that met in the Hague to discuss a political union

Less than 21 years after the end of the First World War, the Second World War broke out in September 1939 when on the third day of that month the United Kingdom and France declared war on Germany, which had invaded Poland two days earlier. The Second World War would last for nearly six years (although some historians consider the war to have started in Asia in 1937), and all of Europe was ravaged. The Allies, principally the United States, Great Britain, France, and the Soviet Union, emerged as victors, while the Axis Powers, led by Germany and Japan (Italy had surrendered to the Allies in 1943) were defeated.

After two world wars that had decimated the continent of Europe in little more than thirty years, leading politicians believed that a supranational body needed to be created to bring a permanent form of peace to Europe. After the First World War, there was a failed attempt led by US President Woodrow Wilson to create a global League of Nations. After the Second World War, in 1945, the intercontinental organization designed to bring peace and security to the world, the United Nations, was established. However, those in Europe wanted to create a pan-European movement due to European countries' historical, cultural, economic, and social ties. Such a union of European countries would also make it easier to for the United States to administer aid to the countries it had agreed to financially help with the Marshall Plan.

The origins of the European Union started with a bilateral treaty signed by France and Britain in 1947. Through a number of treaties, the alliance among Western European countries grew in strength and power to encompass economic, political, and social ideals. The first formal organization, the European Coal and Steel Community comprising six countries, gave way to the more cohesive organization the European Economic Community, which in turn was a forebear to the European Union. During this evolution the European confederate project continued to grow in geographical size, economic cohesion, and shared political beliefs. Today, the European Union now has 27 member countries and a population of nearly 450 million, with shared political institutions, a common economic market, an international currency in circulation in the majority of member states, and a commitment to peace, democracy, justice, and human rights.

The European Union: The History of the Political and Economic Union of Europe's Nations after World War II examines how the various attempts to forge a union came together after the war and led to the current EU. Along with pictures of important people, places, and events, you will learn about the EU like never before.

Plotting a New World Order

Separated by vast gulfs of political, cultural, and philosophical divergence, the three chief Allied nations of World War II – the United States, the Soviet Union, and Great Britain – attempted to formulate a joint policy through a series of three conferences during and immediately after the conflict. The second meeting, named the Yalta Conference after its Black Sea venue, occurred in February 1945 and was both the most well-known and most influential of them all.

Adolf Hitler's Third Reich had scant time remaining when the "Big Three" met to discuss the future of Germany, Europe, and the postwar world as a whole. No doubt existed regarding the war's outcome; the Americans had shattered the Wehrmacht's desperate last throw in the west, the Ardennes Offensive, during the Battle of the Bulge in the weeks immediately preceding Yalta, and the Soviet front lay just 50 miles east of Berlin, with the Red Army preparing for its final push into the Reich's capital after a successful surprise winter campaign.

Among the agreements, the Conference called for Germany's unconditional surrender, the split of Berlin, and German demilitarization and reparations. Stalin, Churchill and Roosevelt also discussed the status of Poland, and Russian involvement in the United Nations. By this time Stalin had thoroughly established Soviet authority in most of Eastern Europe and made it clear that he had no intention of giving up lands his soldiers had fought and died for. The best he would offer Churchill and Roosevelt was the promise that he would allow free elections to be held. He made it clear, though, that the only acceptable outcome to any Polish election would be one that supported communism. One Allied negotiator would later describe Stalin's very formidable negotiating skills. "Marshal Stalin as a negotiator was the toughest proposition of all. Indeed, after something like thirty years' experience of international conferences of one kind and another, if I had to pick a team for going into a conference room, Stalin would be my first choice. Of course the man was ruthless and of course he knew his purpose. He never wasted a word. He never stormed, he was seldom even irritated."

The final question lay in what to do with a conquered Germany. Both the Western Allies and Stalin wanted Berlin, and knew that whoever held the most of it when the truce was signed would end up controlling the city. Thus they spent the next several months pushing their generals further and further toward this goal, but the Russians got there first. Thus, when the victorious allies met in Potsdam in 1945, it remained Britain and America's task to convince Stalin to divide the country, and even the city, between them. They accomplished this, but at a terrible cost: Russia got liberated Austria.

Given its context and importance, the Yalta Conference represented a contentious matter in its own day, and it remains so among historians both professional and amateur. As just one example, while some lauded Roosevelt's political dexterity, many others viewed him as excessively naïve in his dealings with Stalin, or even as a pro-communist quisling.

Furthermore, while the representatives of the chief Allied powers made important decisions at Yalta, they did not divide Europe at that time. The exact future of Europe remained fluid, only coalescing in a more familiar Cold War form during and after the Potsdam Conference following Germany's defeat. In fact, the actual strategic situation, with its iron, deterministic logic of military power, cut across the hopes and intentions of the participants. The West wanted Eastern Europe freed and democratic once again, but Stalin already owned it and mustered hundreds of divisions to enforce his ownership. The Russians wanted Germany but the Anglo-American offensive would likely engulf most of it before the Soviets broke through the final defenses of the dying Wehrmacht.

Thus, the Yalta Conference proved mostly futile, with the sole exception of establishing the United Nations, at Roosevelt's insistence. The nine agreements that Stalin, Churchill, and Roosevelt signed at the end of the Conference used trumpeting phrases about freedom, peace, and brotherhood, but they contained no practical or actionable content. These documents temporarily papered over the fact that the shape of postwar Europe would be decided not by reasoned arguments, but by the fierce, undeniable logic of shells, bullets, tanks, and aircraft.

Yalta neither delayed nor created the Cold War; the collision between two utterly incompatible systems of thought – one that, despite its flaws, placed its faith in freedom, human rights, and majority rule, and the other that believed in paranoid dictatorship enforced through systematic state violence and terror – seemed inevitable either way. If anything, Yalta enabled the three leaders to project a momentary phantasm of unity, permitting them to postpone their intractable hostility for a few months in order to first defeat Germany.

Churchill, Roosevelt, and Stalin at the Yalta Conference

The outcome of the Yalta Conference remains highly controversial in interpretations of World War II. Some praise the Western Allies for winning more than they might otherwise have through adroit negotiation with the aggressive Soviet state. Others condemn Roosevelt as either a naïve fool or even a sort of quisling, failing to counter Stalin's demands and thus abandoning Eastern Europe to its fate as the footstool of the relentless Stalinist empire.

In fact, though evidence can be combed from the records to support multiple viewpoints, the most plausible explanation remains that the Yalta Conference proved largely futile mostly because little room for discussion existed. Stalin already held most the territory his country would retain mastery over until the dissolution of the Soviet Union. With such a strong position – basically unassailable, with the Red Army built up afresh by massive Lend-Lease aid and domestic production, and honed to a relatively professional force – the Soviet leader had no reason to yield an inch on Poland or the rest of Eastern Europe, and in fact he did not. Roosevelt and Churchill simply had no leverage at all to compel Stalin to restore the freedom of his new client states. They could offer little the Soviets did not already have, and with the Third Reich still actively at war, they could not risk a full breach with Stalin that might (as they believed) cause the two mustached dictators to unite again. Short of declaring war on the Soviet Union and defeating it in an extensive battle, the American and British heads of state had no options to induce Stalin's compliance.

With characteristic astuteness, the translator Charles Bohlen summed up the untenable position of the Western Allies succinctly: "I do not presume to know what was going on in Roosevelt's mind, but from what he said at Yalta [...] I feel that he did everything he could to help the Poles. [...] The compromise failed because Stalin insisted on more than security against attack; he wanted to establish the Soviet system of authoritarian control of every aspect of life in Poland. The Red Army gave Stalin the power he needed to carry out his wishes, regardless of his promises at Yalta. Stalin held all the cards and played them well. Eventually, we had to throw in our hand."

One other disadvantage hampered the Western Allies' negotiations. Their accounts inadvertently reveal them, despite their political acumen, as basically honest men. They tended to want to believe the best of Stalin and the Soviets, taking gestures of friendliness at face value. Both, particularly Roosevelt, overlooked signs of Soviet hostility, believing Stalin to be a "good fellow" at bottom, one who liked them and wanted to reach a mutually beneficial understanding.

While remembering expediency and showing skill and even occasional duplicity working within their own democratic systems, they still showed clearly that they came from a relatively civilized political climate. They showed comparatively open and trusting personalities, and a reflexive assumption that their their Soviet counterpart would, to some degree at least, "play fair." Both men had limits they would not pass.

Stalin, the product of a murderous revolution and an even more murderous dictatorship who survived and reigned through treachery, brutality, and terror among the violent, deadly men comprising the Soviet power structure, wielded a cunning his more forthright Western counterparts proved ill-equipped to match. The Soviet dictator had overseen a state founded on mass executions, torture, prison camps, assassination, engineered famine, and the utter dominance of the state over every facet of public and private life. He recognized no limits to his actions; he aimed to win, and he applied all his considerable cunning to achieving this goal.

Furthermore, he hated the two men he dealt with venomously, despite his outward show of friendliness. One of his rants to Yugoslav communist leader Milovan Djilas in 1944 revealed his true loathing of Roosevelt and Churchill as the caricatured representatives of a capitalist system he wholly demonized and wished to destroy: "Perhaps you think that just because we are the allies of the English we have forgotten who they are [...] And Churchill? Churchill is the kind who, if you don't watch him, will slip a kopeck out of your pocket. Yes, a kopeck out of your pocket! By God, a kopeck out of your pocket! And Roosevelt? Roosevelt is not like that. He dips in his hand only for bigger coins. But Churchill? Churchill—even for a kopeck." (Plokhy, 2010, 84).

Finally, it's important to remember that the Western Allies still lacked the powerful bargaining chip of nuclear weapons. The atom bomb remained several months in the future, and even Roosevelt's staff had skepticism that it would ever work. In fact, Truman's decision to drop two bombs on Japan may have been partly an effort to redress the imbalance of power between the Soviet Union and the West inherited from the Yalta Conference. Truman certainly used the threat of nuclear power adroitly a few years later, successfully bluffing the belligerent Soviet Union with a list of 30 major Soviet cities chosen for nuclear annihilation at a point in time when America possessed only 8 nuclear bombs.

Either way, while Yalta represented an overall failure for Roosevelt and Churchill on most matters, the force of circumstance could not make it otherwise. Stalin held the high ground on most of the matters under discussion and, unsurprisingly, emerged with most of the territories and concessions he wanted, since he already enjoyed possession of them.

Churchill tried to save the British Empire and ultimately failed, but Roosevelt did manage one striking diplomatic success in the establishment of the United Nations, a body that has continued to influence global affairs into the 21st century, over 70 years after the Yalta Conference concluded.

The Potsdam Conference brought together the leaders of the three major Allied powers for the last time at the end of World War II and at the threshold of the Cold War. A follow up to the Yalta Conference just five months earlier, Potsdam attempted to work out the contours of the postwar world.

Though it came so shortly after Yalta, the Potsdam Conference also highlighted a turnover of leadership on the world stage. British Prime Minister Winston Churchill, who gave his nation hope in the darkest days of World War II, had suffered a stunning defeat at the hands of the Labor candidate Clement Attlee, who replaced him towards the end of the Conference. President Franklin Delano Roosevelt died prior to the meeting, leading to his replacement by the new president Harry S. Truman, a keen-minded pragmatist whose intense focus on America's advantage contrasted with Roosevelt's internationalism. Only General Secretary Josef Stalin, dictator of the Soviet Union, remained unchanged from the earlier summit. Destined to continue in power for another 8 years until his death (possibly at the hands of Lavrenty Beria), the Russian strongman found himself confronting a world in which the United States possessed the atomic bomb.

At the same time, despite the power of the central personalities, their lieutenants also played a role at Potsdam. James Byrnes, Truman's right-hand man at the conference, concealed a deeply astute, intelligent, and cunning mind under the exterior of a scrawny country bumpkin. Fleet Admiral William D. Leahy provided continuity with the Yalta conference for the American delegation, while Vyacheslav Molotov and Foreign Minister Anthony Eden also reprised their roles from the earlier summit.

World War II was so horrific that in its aftermath, the victorious Allies sought to address every aspect of it to both punish war criminals and attempt to ensure that there was never a conflict like it again. World War II was unprecedented in terms of the global scale of the fighting, the number of both civilian and military casualties, the practice of total war, and war crimes. World War II also left two undisputed, ideologically opposed superpowers standing, shaping global politics over the last 65 years.

Though the countries had often discussed Russia joining America and Britain's fight against the Japanese, it became clear at Potsdam that this was not going to happen. Instead, Stalin pleaded for help for his own country, which had been decimated by the fighting with Germany. Russia had lost more than 30,000 factories and so much farm land that the vast majority of the population was suffering from malnutrition. Stalin was also particularly concerned that the Allies might stage an invasion of Russia and overthrow his regime. While it may have seemed at the time that he was just being paranoid, it is now known that George Patton was already pushing Truman and the other world leaders to go ahead and finish the weakened Soviets off, meaning Stalin might actually have been wise to build up communist governments in Czechoslovakia, East Germany, Bulgaria and elsewhere.

The Allies managed to agree on the need for an international war crimes tribunal to bring the perpetrators of Nazi mass murders to justice. The British – first Churchill, and then Attlee carrying on his policy – argued for Nuremberg as the site of the trials. The symbolic intention would, the Allies hoped, impress itself on the German mind. The Nazi Party's infamous rallies occurred in that city during the years of the Third Reich, and the Allied leaders all agreed to that venue on the 31st.

Despite this agreement, the Soviets set up their own trials in Poland and elsewhere. The fate of Rudolf Hess, Hitler's nominal second in command who flew to England early in the war on a quixotic mission to arrange an alliance between the British and the Third Reich, also came to the surface at Potsdam. His name found its way onto a list of the 10 war criminals selected as the symbolic representation of the rest for diplomatic purposes.

Hess

The Allies also agreed not to dismember Germany, a matter Truman considered particularly important. The American president believed the current war sprang largely from the punitive terms inflicted on the Germans after World War I, and he did not want portions of Germany openly detached to cause problems again in the future. The division of the country into two parts, East and West Germany, represented a de facto dismemberment, but the vast majority of Germany remained united, giving it the necessary territory for recovery and avoidance of Truman's fears on that score. The expulsion of the ethnic Germans from the section of territory given to Poland proved grimly effective in quashing any unrest there, since it created ethnic homogeneity in the new Polish state and consequent relative stability.

The Soviet Union had no qualms in accepting Chiang Kai-Shek's Nationalists in China as part of the postwar order, though of course the Russians scooped off some territorial acquisitions. The Soviets also invaded Manchuria immediately after the Potsdam Conference, and they continued their attack into the Kurile Islands for several days after the Japanese formally surrendered, interested in pushing their borders out as far as possible.

Chiang Kai-Shek

In the matter of Iran, which the Americans used as a Lend-Lease route into the Soviet Union during the war, Stalin agreed to withdraw Soviet troops, to the immense relief of the Shah. Truman also stated his intention to remove all American troops within 60 days to send them to the Pacific Theater, leading Stalin to remark, "So as to rid the United States of any worries we promise you that no action will be taken by us against Iran." (Feis, 1960, 304).

The final plenary sessions on August 1st ended on a terse and sour note. First, Stalin and Truman agreed, and Attlee rubber-stamped, a division of Germany (and Europe) based on the actually existing military frontiers. The Soviet Union kept what it controlled, and the rest of Europe would remain free, with the United States administering West Germany in conjunction with the British until a proper civil government established itself.

Truman raised the issue of his international waterways again, but Stalin abruptly and angrily rejected the idea. In doing so, he spoke the only English words anyone heard him enunciate at the conference: "No. I say no."

Attlee made a feeble effort to assist the royalists in Greece as part of the agreement, since they currently found themselves embroiled in a struggle with communist insurgents. However, he was soon forced to abandon the struggle, with the Greek anti-communists left on their own until Truman came to their aid in 1947. The British Chiefs of Staff told Attlee, "In our view the defence of the Greek frontier must be left to the Greek forces and later guaranteed by the world security organization [...] In [the] absence of American troops in Greece we cannot entertain the idea of unilateral British military action in [the] Balkans." (Thomas-Symonds, 2010, 146).

After effectively agreeing to the status quo in Europe, Truman and Stalin parted for the final time late on August 1st. The Potsdam Protocol recognized these facts and stated the need for another summit in the near future, a summit that would never take place. Loathing foreign travel, Truman suggested that the follow up summit should gather in Washington, D.C., to which the atheistic Soviet dictator answered, "God willing."

On the evening of July 31st, Truman saw that the negotiations finally drew towards their conclusion. With only one day remaining in the Potsdam Conference (to the president's immense relief), he prepared written orders to be transmitted back to the United States regarding the use of the first two atom bombs against Japan. He included a terse but clear injunction about the timing of the new weapons' deployment: "Release when ready but not sooner than August 2."

A picture of President Truman ordering the use of the atomic bomb

The European Coal and Steel Community

In 1946, speaking to a war-weary world, Winston Churchill sounded what would become a famous warning about the aggression of the Soviet Union and the dangers of communism's spread while speaking to a group of college students at Westminster College in Fulton, Missouri: "I am sure you would wish me to state the facts as I see them to you, to place before you certain facts about the present position in Europe. From Stettin in the Baltic to Trieste in the Adriatic, an iron curtain has descended across the Continent. Behind that line lie all the capitals of the ancient states of Central and Eastern Europe. Warsaw, Berlin, Prague, Vienna, Budapest, Belgrade, Bucharest and Sofia, all these famous cities and the populations around them lie in what I must call the Soviet sphere, and all are subject in one form or another, not only to Soviet influence but to a very high and, in many cases, increasing measure of control from Moscow."[1]

---

[1] Churchill, Winston. "The Sinews of Peace." Westminster College. Mississippi, Fulton. 5 Mar. 1946. *The Churchill Centre*. Web. 2 Feb. 2015.

This "border" of states, the protection that Stalin claimed he needed to ensure his country's post-war security, included "Poland, Czechoslovakia, Hungary, Bulgaria, Romania, and the Soviet Occupation Zone in East Germany."[2] These areas would develop into Soviet satellite states, relying on the Soviet's for military defense, serving as the Soviet industrial plans' source for natural resources, and experiencing occasional crackdowns for showing signs of independence or unrest over the next 40 plus years.

That same year, on September 19, 1946, Churchill delivered a speech at the University of Zurich calling for the creation of a "United States of Europe." Referring to the failure of the proposed League of Nations after the First World War, Churchill stated that the opportunity to unite nations in the aftermath of yet another world war must not be forsaken. Such a "United States of Europe" would be essential to ensure that hundreds of millions of people could be "happy and free, prosperous and safe."[3] Fundamental to this union, according to Churchill, was a partnership between France and Germany. The former leader also championed the creation of a Council of Europe, a body that came into being in 1949 and still exists today, albeit separately from the European Union and with a primary focus on human rights, democracy, and the rule of law rather than economics or a trade union, although the two bodies are not mutually exclusive.

The first formal treaty signed in the post-war period was the Treaty of Dunkirk on March 4, 1947, a bilateral treaty with the two signatories being Britain and France. It included the proviso that the two countries would work in alliance to "prevent Germany from becoming a menace again."[4] This treaty was significant because it increased confidence within France, gave encouragement to the smaller Western European states, and demonstrated to the United States that two large Western European countries had laid the groundwork to start working together.[5] This prepared the ground for the Treaty of Brussels 1948, encouraged the United States to participate in an Atlantic Alliance, and was a precursor to the first meeting between the European states which would become recipients of the United States' Marshall Plan, otherwise known as the European Recovery Program, a financial aid stimulus package.

The Treaty of Brussels, also known as the Brussels Pact, was signed by the United Kingdom, France, the Netherlands, Belgium, and Luxembourg on March 17, 1948. Notable for codifying an alliance between five Western European countries, the treaty stated its aims, including the following: "To reaffirm their faith in fundamental human rights, in the dignity and worth of the human person and in the other ideals proclaimed in the Charter of the United Nations; To fortify and preserve the principles of democracy, personal freedom and political liberty, the constitutional traditions and the rule of law, which are their common heritage; To strengthen, with these aims in view, the economic, social and cultural ties by which they are already united;

---

[2] Rottman, 5.

[3] Winston Churchill, "Winston Churchill's Speech" (speech, University of Zurich, Zurich, September 19, 1946).

[4] John Baylis, "Britain and the Dunkirk Treaty: The Origins of NATO," *Journal of Strategic Studies* 5 no. 2 (1982): 244.

[5] Baylis, "Britain and the Dunkirk Treaty," 244.

To cooperate loyally and to coordinate their efforts to create in Western Europe a firm basis for European economic recovery; To afford assistance to each other, in accordance with the Charter of the United Nations, in maintaining international peace and security and in resisting any policy of aggression; To take such steps as may be held to be necessary in the event of a renewal by Germany of a policy of aggression; To associate progressively in the pursuance of these aims other States inspired by the same ideals and animated by the like determination; Desiring for these purposes to conclude a treaty for collaboration in economic, social and cultural matters and for collective self-defence."[6]

The signatories were still wary of possible German aggression because West Germany (the Federal Republic of Germany [FRG]) and East Germany (the German Democratic Republic [GDR]) did not formally come into being until 1949, so at the time of the signing of the Treaty of Brussels there was no "West Germany," then still under the supreme authority of the commanders-in-chiefs in Germany of the United Kingdom, France, and the United States.

The Treaty of Brussels was discussed with a wider audience at the Hague Conference, a four-day meeting lasting from May 7-10, 1948, which was attended by delegates from all parts of the political spectrum as well as by philosophers, journalists, academics, religious leaders, and entrepreneurs. There were even delegates from countries behind the "Iron Curtain," since exiled in Western Europe, who attended.[7] The agreements included commitments to human rights, economic, social and cultural ties, economic recovery, international peace and security, and the possibility of other European countries joining this alliance.

In 1948 and 1949 two further international bodies were established, although they were not direct precursors of the European Coal and Steel Community (1952), which is viewed as the entity which led to the European Community and later to the European Union. The first of these bodies was the Organization for European Economic Cooperation (OEEC)[8]. Formed in 1948, it was established in response to the Marshall Plan and for the purpose of continuing to work on a joint economic and infrastructure rebuilding recovery plan. The OEEC promoted cooperation between the member countries, developed intra-European trade by reducing tariffs and other barriers to the expansion of trade, and studied the feasibility of creating a free trade area, among other aims.[9] Unlike the Treaty of Brussels, the OEEC had 18 participants when it was established, coming from most parts of Europe free from Soviet control and including the future West Germany. The OEEC went into decline in 1952 due to the end of the Marshall Plan and the emergence of the North Atlantic Treaty Organization (NATO).

---

[6] The Brussels Treaty, Mar. 17, 1948, AE TC 365.

[7] Wilfred Loth. *Building Europe: A History of European Unification* (Berlin: De Gruyter Oldenbourg, 2015), 13.

[8] The OEEC is now the OECD which now includes includes 37 countries. They include Australia, New Zealand, Japan, South Korea, Turkey, Mexico, and Chile.

[9] "Organisation for European Economic Co-operation, OECD, accessed March 26, 2020, http://www.oecd.org/general/organisationforeuropeaneconomicco-operation.htm

The second international body that was established in 1949 and was not a forerunner of the European Union but did embody some of the European Union's values was the Council of Europe. The Council of Europe was founded by 10 member states which had had representatives in attendance at the Hague Conference. In addition to the five signatories of the Treaty of Brussels, Ireland, Italy, Denmark, Norway, and Sweden were also founding members.[10] The Council of Europe's first formal convention focused on human rights, although it also reached its objectives through "agreements and common action in economic, social, cultural, scientific, legal and administrative matters and in the maintenance and further realisation of human rights and fundamental freedoms."[11] The Council of Europe is still in existence today – a separate but complementary entity to the European Union.

The Treaty of Paris was signed on April 18, 1951 and came into force on July 23, 1952. This treaty established the European Coal and Steel Community (ECSC) and is seen as the first formal forerunner of the European Union. The six signatories were: France, West Germany, Italy, Belgium, the Netherlands, and Luxembourg.[12] The United Kingdom, up until this point an important participant in the promotion of Western European integration, did not sign. Unlike the six signatory countries, the UK had particularly close ties to the United States and the Commonwealth countries. With American support, the United Kingdom objected to calls for the Federal Republic of Germany to become a full member of the ECSC as well as to some of the economic policies put forward by the future ECSC countries.[13] The British Foreign Secretary, Ernest Bevin, vetoed the terms put forward by the ECSC's Consultative Committee. The British viewed the proposals as being not just economic but also political, and did not want to compromise the UK's standing with the United States and Commonwealth countries.

By 1950, it could be foreseen that the financial aid given by the Marshall Plan would soon end. Additionally, in April of that year it was known that Dean Acheson, the U.S. Secretary of State, and Ernest Bevin, the British Foreign Secretary, would be in attendance at a meeting in West Germany alongside the French Foreign Minister, where it would be proposed to limit the restrictions on West German steel production. Occupation of West Germany by these three former Allies would also be reduced. Robert Schuman, the French Foreign Minister, took advantage of these circumstances to propose a supranational coal and steel authority between the French and Germans which would exclude the British.[14] After consultation with Italy, the Netherlands, Belgium, and Luxembourg, a joint communiqué was issued in June 1950 signalling all six countries' general agreement with Schuman's plan.[15] This was later formalized by the Treaty of Paris.

---

[10] "About the Council of Europe – Overview," Council of Europe, accessed March 26, 2020, https://www.coe.int/en/web/yerevan/the-coe/about-coe/overview

[11] Council of Europe, "About the Council of Europe – Overview."

[12] Treaty Establishing the European Coal and Steel Community, April 18, 1951, auteur: x.

[13] Loth, *Building* Europe, 27-28.

[14] Loth, *Building Europe,* 31.

[15] Loth, *Building Europe,* 33.

Acheson

Schuman

The treaty establishing the ECSC placed heavy emphasis on world peace and economic development:

> CONSIDERING that world peace may be safeguarded only by creative efforts equal to the dangers which menace it;
>
> CONVINCED that the contribution which an organized and vital Europe can bring to civilization is indispensable to the maintenance of peaceful relations;
>
> CONSCIOUS of the fact that Europe can be built only by concrete actions which create a real solidarity and by the establishment of common bases for economic development; 'DESIROUS of assisting through the expansion of their basic production in raising the standard of living and in furthering the works of peace;

RESOLVED to substitute for historic rivalries a fusion of their essential interests; to establish, by creating an economic community, the foundation of a broad and independent community among peoples long divided by bloody conflicts; and to lay the bases of institutions capable of giving direction to their future common destiny;

HAVE DECIDED to create a European Coal and Steel Community.[16]

Despite the fact that the name of the treaty refers to coal and steel, the treaty itself goes further and establishes a precursor to a Common Market covering much of economic activity.[17]

A map of the six member countries of the ECSC (at the time, Algeria was a part of the Fourth French Republic)

The Treaty of Paris also established a High Authority, a Common Assembly, a Special Council composed of Ministers, and a Court of Justice.[18] The High Authority acted as the ECSC's executive, independent from the member states, and included a President and Vice-President chosen from the members of the High Authority. The Common Assembly acted as a legislature, and its members were chosen by the Parliaments of each member state. The Common Assembly had supervisory powers over the High Authority. The Special Council also comprised members chosen by the Parliaments of the member states, but the Special Council's role was to "harmonize" the actions of the High Authorities and the member states, which were still

---

[16] Treaty Establishing the European Coal and Steel Community, April 18, 1951, auteur: x, 3.

[17] Treaty Establishing the European Coal and Steel Community, April 18, 1951, auteur: x, 4.

[18] Treaty Establishing the European Coal and Steel Community, April 18, 1951, auteur: x, 6.

responsible for the general economic policies of their own countries.[19] The Special Council had its own President and was responsible for setting the salaries, allowances, and pensions of the High Authority and other high-level functionaries. The High Authority acted independently of the member states and it was the role of the Special Council to ensure that the High Authority's decisions could be and would be respected by the member states. Finally, the Court of Justice acted as the ECSC's judicial branch. The Court had jurisdiction to listen to appeals made by either member states or the Special Council for the annulment of decisions made by the High Authority.

In such a set-up it can be seen that a set of "checks and balances," similar to those that form the United States Constitution, was established among the higher authorities of the ECSC. Member states maintained the right to choose the members of the Common Assembly and Special Council, as well as appeal against the decisions of the High Authority.

The legacy of the ECSC is mixed. The ECSC was not successful in controlling the power of the iron and steel producers in Europe, with West Germany establishing dominance and the French failing to rationalize until it was too late; no definition of a common coal policy was ever truly reached; equalization of pay among the member countries was never reached; and price agreements were never abolished. Steel- and iron-masters were able to continue to fix real prices.[20] Oil, gas, and electricity emerged as competitors to coal, and the ECSC failed to deliver a comprehensive oil strategy. However, the ECSC was able to reduce the price of steel which led to further investment. The ECSC's real gains were in terms of welfare. Funding was provided so that over 15 years more than 100,000 workers were able to buy their own apartments. When coal or steel workers lost their jobs, the ECSC was able to pay for approximately 50% of their redeployment costs in addition to granting aid so that these regions could be redeveloped. ECSC investments meant that approximately 100,000 new jobs were created, with around one-third of these going to unemployed coal and steel workers.[21]

The ECSC only lasted five years as the predominant supranational European organization. Energy crises (the Suez Canal crisis of 1956-57, which saw the British and the French fail in their effort to maintain control of the Suez Canal in Egypt which was the means to transport oil to Europe, and the emergence of the use of atomic energy for domestic and commercial use since the end of the Second World War) meant that there was less emphasis on coal as an energy source. In 1954, there had been a failure to establish a European Defense Community, which led to a modification of the terms of the Brussels Treaty.[22] As a result, Johan Willem Beyen, the Dutch Foreign Minister, and Paul-Henri Spaak, his Belgian counterpart, wanted to move the

---

[19] Treaty Establishing the European Coal and Steel Community, April 18, 1951, auteur: x, 12.

[20] Gilbert Mathieu, "The History of the ECSC: Good Times and Bad," *Le Monde*, May 9, 1970, https://www.cvce.eu/en/obj/the_history_of_the_ecsc_good_times_and_bad_from_le_monde_9_may_1970-en-54f09b32-1b0c-4060-afb3-5e475dcafda8.html.

[21] Mathieu, "The History of the ECSC."

[22] Loth, *Building Europe,* 52.

focus of the ECSC away from defense matters, redefine its political scope, address new energy needs, and concentrate on a strong customs union and a more competitive market.[23] Beyen and Spaak called for a further conference to address these issues. At this stage, the Benelux countries (Belgium, the Netherlands, and Luxembourg) were more in favor of European economic integration than West Germany's Chancellor, Konrad Adenauer, or French Prime Minister Guy Mollett. The French wanted to contain West Germany's ability to produce atomic weapons, while Germany feared that the French would not agree to a Common Market, so preferred to focus on Euratom, the proposal for a European Atomic Energy Community (EAEC).[24] These were matters that had to be thrashed out over the next two years, led by the initiatives of the Benelux ministers.

Beyen

---

[23] Pierre-Henri Laurent, "Paul-Henri Spaak and the Diplomatic Origins of the Common Market, 1955-1956," *Political Science Quarterly* 85 no. 3 (1970): 373-374.

[24] Jeffrey Vanke. "The Treaty of Rome and Europeanism" *The Journal of the Historical Society* 7 no. 4 (2007): 457-460.

Spaak

At the Messina Conference on June 1-2, 1955, Spaak was charged with leading the Spaak Committee, which had a brief to further investigate deepening what would become a common economic market. At this conference, the six member states of the ECSC agreed on proposals for: 'the elimination of customs duties between Member States, the establishment of an external Common Customs Tariff, the introduction of common policies for agriculture and transport, the creation of a European Social Fund, the establishment of a European Investment Bank, [and] the development of closer relations between the Member States.'[25] These proposals would be enacted into law in the Treaty of Rome of 1957, which provided for the establishment of the European Economic Community (EEC) and the European Atomic Energy Community.

The Venice Conference took place on May 29-30, 1956 to discuss the findings that the Spaak Committee had been tasked with investigating the previous year. The main topics under discussion were the creation of a full Common Market as well as a body to regulate atomic energy among member states. Terms were agreed by the six member states, and one month later

---

[25] European Parliament, *The Historical Development of European Integration* (Brussels, 2018), 4.

the Intergovernmental Conference on the Common Market and Euratom was convened, a conference at which terms were thrashed out which directly led to signing of the Treaty of Rome the following year. (The separate treaty which authorized the creation of the European Atomic Energy Committee, the Euratom Treaty, was signed on the same day as the Treaty of Rome).

The Original Six Members of the European Economic Community

On March 25, 1957, the Treaty of Rome was signed and the European Economic Community officially came into being on January 1, 1958. Although involved in discussions, the British spurned the chance to join the Common Market, citing the strength of its international bonds to the Commonwealth and the United States; the UK did not want membership of a European Common Market to supersede its economic relationships with its former and current colonies.[26] The six European countries that signed the Treaty of Rome desired European peace and prosperity, although not at the expense of replacing the nation-state. Given that Germany had been the main threat to European peace, the inclusion of West Germany was seen to be the best way to assure future peaceful co-existence.[27]

While the Treaty of Paris established the ECSC, which was an agreement to work towards integration[28], the Treaty of Rome brought this integration to fruition in the shape of the European Economic Community. The six signatory countries declared themselves to be:

> DETERMINED to establish the foundations of an ever closer union among the European peoples;
>
> DECIDED to ensure the economic and social progress of their countries by common action in eliminating the barriers which divide Europe;
>
> DIRECTING their efforts to the essential purpose of constantly improving the living and working conditions of their peoples;
>
> RECOGNISING that the removal of existing obstacles calls for concerted action in order to guarantee a steady expansion, a balanced trade and fair competition;
>
> ANXIOUS to strengthen the unity of their economies and to ensure their harmonious development by reducing the differences existing between the various regions and by mitigating the backwardness of the less favoured;
>
> DESIROUS of contributing by means of a common commercial policy to the progressive abolition of restrictions on international trade;

---

[26] Vanke, "The Treaty of Rome and Europeanism," 466.
[27] Vanke, "The Treaty of Rome and Europeanism," 477.
[28] European Parliament, *The Historical Development of European Integration*, 3.

INTENDING to confirm the solidarity which binds Europe and overseas countries, and desiring to ensure the development of their prosperity, in accordance with the principles of the Charter of the United Nations; [and]

RESOLVED to strengthen the safeguards of peace and liberty by establishing this combination of resources, and calling upon the other peoples of Europe who share their ideal to join in their efforts.[29]

The Treaty of Rome established the Common Market of the EEC. Wide-ranging aspects of a common economic policy were detailed in the treaty. Customs duties and quantitative restrictions were removed from all goods imported or exported between the member countries. All six nations stated that they would adopt a common customs tariff and commercial policy to be applied towards third countries. Freedom of movement of persons, services and capital was also authorized, meaning that citizens of one country could live and work in any of the other five signatory countries. A Common Agricultural Policy and a Common Transport Policy were set out. A European Social Fund was created to improve employment possibilities for workers and to help raise their standard of living. While the member states would maintain their national banks and treasuries, a supranational European Investment Bank was established to facilitate the new Community's economic expansion via newly created resources. The Treaty of Rome also made provision for more member states to join the EEC in the future.[30]

EEC social policy was also laid out in the Treaty of Rome. This established common rules surrounding "employment, labor legislation and working conditions, occupational and continuation training, social security, protection against occupational accidents and diseases, industrial hygiene, the law as to trade unions, and collective bargaining between employers and workers."[31] This was not to say that member states could not determine their own individual regulations with regards to the above, but that minimum EEC standards had to be met. Equal pay for men and women was also enshrined in the Treaty of Rome.[32]

The institutions that would govern the work of the EEC were the Assembly, the Council, the Commission, and the Court of Justice. The Assembly, consisting of members to be chosen by the Parliaments of their respective states, held advisory, deliberative and supervisory powers. The Assembly could deliberate on and propose amendments to draft budgets that were submitted to it by the Council. The Assembly also had the power to issue opinions on certain regulations that were referred to it by the Commission or the Council. As established in the Treaty of Rome, West Germany, France, and Italy could name 36 members to the Assembly; the Netherlands and Belgium were able to name 14 representatives; and Luxembourg had six members participating in the Assembly.[33]

---

[29] Treaty Establishing the European Economic Community, March 25, 1957, [s.d. 378 p], 3.
[30] Treaty Establishing the European Economic Community, March 25, 1957, [s.d. 378 p].
[31] Treaty Establishing the European Economic Community, March 25, 1957, [s.d. 378 p], 45.
[32] Treaty Establishing the European Economic Community, March 25, 1957, [s.d. 378 p], 46.

The Council comprised six members, one from each state, chosen by the national governments. The common economic policy was administered by the Council, which also had decision-making power in most cases. The Council had the power to ask the Commission to undertake studies deemed "desirable for the achievement of common objectives"[34] and then act on the Commission's proposals.

The Commission consisted of nine members appointed by the member state governments to ensure that the provisions of the Treaty were being carried out. The members of the Commission could not seek or accept instructions from the government of any member state.[35] The Commission presented proposals to the Council (which could only be amended by a unanimous vote from the Council), made recommendations, and delivered opinions. Both the Commission and the Council held executive powers and frequently collaborated with each other, the main difference between the two being that the Council was responsible for executing the common economic policy while the Commission ensured that the Articles of the Treaty were adhered to.

The fourth institution that carried out the work of the EEC was the Court of Justice which was composed of seven judges. The Court of Justice held the EEC's judicial powers, ensuring that law was observed in the interpretation and application of the Treaty. The Court of Justice was able to assess the legality of the Council's and the Commission's actions.[36] If a member state felt that another member state was not complying with the terms of the Treaty, it could refer the matter to the Court of Justice. Similarly, if any state was found by the Commission not to be heeding the terms of the Treaty, this state could be referred to the Court of Justice by the Commission.[37]

In addition to the four main EEC institutions, the Treaty of Rome also provided for an advisory body, the Economic and Social Committee (ESC). Consisting of individuals who were producers, farmers, workers, transport operators, craftsmen and [from the] professional occupations, the ESC had a consultative status.[38] This advisory body was meant to represent the various categories of the EEC's economic and social life.

Despite the fact that the functions of the EEC institutions had been clearly laid out in the Treaty of Rome, there was still confusion in 1958 as to the exact role of the European Commission.[39] The Treaty thus far had the character of a "framework agreement" and the customs union was to be realized gradually.[40] The first President of the European Commission

---

[33] "The EEC Institutions," CVCE.eu, accessed March 27, 2020, https://www.cvce.eu/en/education/unit-content/-/unit/1c8aa583-8ec5-41c4-9ad8-73674ea7f4a7/bd64db50-fa41-4fb1-b3bd-4f99d2cfee2d.
[34] Treaty Establishing the European Economic Community, March 25, 1957, [s.d. 378 p], 51.
[35] Treaty Establishing the European Economic Community, March 25, 1957, [s.d. 378 p], 52.
[36] CVCE.eu, "The EEC Institutions."
[37] Treaty Establishing the European Economic Community, March 25, 1957, [s.d. 378 p], 52.
[38] CVCE.eu, "The EEC Institutions."
[39] Loth, *Building Europe,* 75.
[40] Loth, *Building Europe,* 78.

was the German statesman Walter Hallstein. Hallstein was re-elected three times and served as President from 1958 to 1967. In his capacity as President of the Commission, Hallstein came up with a large number of European policy ideas. Some of his contributions to the advancement of European economic and foreign policy still profoundly shape the European Union today. Early in his presidential career, Hallstein spent a lot of time establishing the Common Agricultural Policy (CAP) in accordance with the EEC Treaty provisions. This led to a need to regulate further economic and financial policy aspects, for example protecting price levels so that member states' currencies would not be devalued by the need to guarantee the free movement of agricultural goods.[41] Hallstein was also a proponent of a currency union to even out developments in the Common Market, an idea which became reality some 30 years later when the Maastricht Treaty was negotiated.

---

[41] Wilhelm Lehman and Christian Salm, *Walter Hallstein: First President of the Commission and Visionary of European Integration*, research Report prepared for the European Parliamentary Research Service, (Luxembourg, 2019), 6.

It was Hallstein's desire to create a "grand administration."[42] Member states had initially dragged their heels at funding the new Community, but Hallstein was able to take advantage of the difficulties in the administrative structuring of the Council and the diminished French interest in European issues owing to domestic political unrest that would lead to the end of the Fourth Republic and the creation of the Fifth Republic. The Commission was able to resolve the division of labor issues, adopt an organizational chart meaning that job positions could be filled, and by the end of 1958 the Commission had nearly one thousand people on its staff and the Budget Committee of the Council of Ministers was up and running.[43] Member states now found themselves faced with a cohesive, functioning Council that was able to force the individual countries to pay their fair share according to the Treaty they had signed up to.

Hallstein also faced difficulties implementing the EEC's free-trade area. Since 1957, the 17 countries in the Organization for European Economic Cooperation had been negotiating a free trade agreement under a committee chaired by a British special minister.[44] The British had decided in 1955 not to join the EEC, just as they had decided not to join the ECSC that preceded it. Britain had hoped to prevent the formation of an economic community of the six ECSC states because at this point in time approximately 50% of Britain's foreign trade was within the Commonwealth, and lower external tariffs signified that imported American and West German industrial products would threaten the exports Britain sent to the EEC.[45] The less stringent economic terms of OEEC membership were viewed more favourably by the British. However, it was not only the British who objected. Other countries too were reluctant to join the Common Market because levels of economic protectionism would be high but at the same time there would not be enough protection from foreign competition.[46] The OEEC's free trade area posed a threat to the EEC's common tariff rate, to the extent of rendering the common tariff obsolete.

When Charles de Gaulle rose to power in France on June 1, 1958 and was charged by constitutional law to draw up a new constitution for France (the Fifth Republic was established on October 4, 1958), he surprised observers by embracing the EEC. Earlier in the 1950s, de Gaulle and most Gaullists had opposed the proposals for a (failed) European Defense Community and Euratom.[47] De Gaulle was a nationalist, and he did not wish to see what he viewed as France's economic, social, or political interests overruled by a supranational organization. However, by 1958 he was willing to work closely with the other EEC leaders to implement the Treaty of Rome, including setting up the Common Agricultural Policy and the

---

[42] Loth, *Building Europe,* 80.
[43] Loth, *Building Europe,* 80.
[44] Loth, *Building Europe,* 83.
[45] Loth, *Building Europe,* 84.
[46] Loth, *Building Europe,* 84.
[47] Andrew Moravcsik, "De Gaulle between Grain and *Grandeur*: The Political Economy of French EC Policy 1958–1970 (Part 1)," *Journal of Cold War Studies* 2 no. 2, (2000): 13.

Common Commercial Policy.[48] De Gaulle was also a realist who understood that by actively participating in the EEC, he could ensure that the superpowers were balanced and Germany could be kept under control. With the leaders of the Fourth Republic that he considered to be "mediocre" now out of power, de Gaulle could now shape France's participation in the EEC as he saw fit.[49]

De Gaulle during World War II

There were two major political issues that arose while Hallstein was President of the European Commission. The first was the United Kingdom's EEC membership application in 1961. The second is what is called the "empty chair" crisis of 1965, when France refused to send representatives to Brussels. With regard to the UK's failed EEC membership bid, this only occurred after seven western European countries (the United Kingdom, Sweden, Denmark, Norway, Switzerland, Austria, and Portugal) agreed to an alternative free trade area, the

---

[48] Moravcsik, "De Gaulle between Grain and *Grandeur* (Part 1)," 4.
[49] Loth, *Building Europe,* 86.

European Free Trade Area (EFTA) on January 4, 1960. Within the EFTA, tariffs on commercial goods imported from other members would be abolished.[50] In response, the EEC decided to accelerate the tariff reductions as a further step to strengthening the Common Market. The creation of the EFTA did not resolve Britain's problems which were caused by the EEC which contained the economies of Germany, France, and Italy, larger than any of the economies that were in the EFTA alongside Britain, and which was growing in strength. The UK did more trade with the EEC states than with the EFTA states, and Britain's trade with the EEC was increasing. Furthermore, trade with the British Commonwealth states was diminishing, and American investors preferred to trade with the EEC rather than the EFTA. Britain was losing competitiveness compared to the EEC states, and the United States was not interested in supporting a bilateral agreement between the EEC and the EFTA.[51] Opinion in British industry, the general public and among experts came to support British entry into the EEC. The Prime Minister, Harold Macmillan, saw the political goal of Britain's entry in the EEC as "to balance de Gaulle now and Germany later."[52]

On August 9, 1961, Britain submitted its application to join the EEC. Hallstein was skeptical. Along with most of the Commission's members, Hallstein believed that UK membership would harm further sectoral integration and eventually lead to a weakened Common Market, because the UK wanted EEC entry on special terms and was unwilling to relinquish any British sovereignty to EEC institutions. Although Hallstein did not possess any real support for Britain entering the EEC, he foresaw that the UK would join the Community one day. Hallstein felt more strongly about the fact that member state governments were conducting accession negotiations with the EEC; he would have preferred that the EEC Commission oversee accession negotiations and he demanded greater powers for the institutions of the EEC.[53]

In contrast to Hallstein's ambivalent attitude towards Britain entering the EEC, de Gaulle was fervently against British membership. By 1962, Harold Macmillan's government was willing to concede to EEC demands regarding economic concessions. De Gaulle continued to oppose British membership and publicly dashed British hopes in January 1963. Even in 1967-1968, a further British attempt to join the EEC was informally vetoed by de Gaulle. The French President did not believe that the British were ready to adopt a truly "European approach."[54] He felt that due to the nature of the British economy, the UK would be likely to block funding for the Common Agricultural Policy, of which France benefited.

The second major political issue that occurred under Hallstein's presidency of the EEC Commission was the "empty chair" crisis. This impasse centered on the wishes of Hallstein and

---

[50] Loth, *Building Europe,* 105.
[51] Loth, *Building Europe,* 105-106.
[52] Loth, *Building Europe,* 106.
[53] Lehman and Salm, *Walter Hallstein,* 7.
[54] Andrew Moravcsik, "De Gaulle between Grain and *Grandeur*: The Political Economy of French EC Policy 1958–1970 (Part 2)," *Journal of Cold War Studies* 2 no. 3, (2000): 6.

de Gaulle. In 1965, discussion was underway in the EEC about the permanent financing arrangements of the Common Agricultural Policy. The CAP was of vital interest to the French, and they sought a system that would not require annual renegotiations. De Gaulle was against adhering to the terms laid out in the Treaty of Rome, but Hallstein believed that under pressure from the other five EEC states, de Gaulle would compromise due to the impending French presidential elections in December 1965 and de Gaulle's need for the French agricultural vote.[55]

However, Hallstein underestimated de Gaulle's resolve. When the June 30 deadline to reach agreement on the Common Agricultural Policy passed, the French government did not ask for more time to negotiate. Instead, de Gaulle ordered the French permanent representative in Brussels to return to Paris. He then declared that the French would boycott future meetings on new EEC policies, resulting in the "empty chair" at the meeting table. As a result, further compromises offered by the Commission were rejected and further discussion of new EEC policies could not take place.[56]

The "empty chair crisis" did not end until six months later with what was called the "Luxembourg Compromise." The Luxembourg Compromise was an extralegal agreement between France and the other five EEC countries that specified that if a particular national government felt that a piece of EEC legislation was threatening to its "vital interest," that government could impede a decision from being taken.[57] This was a considerable victory for de Gaulle at Hallstein's expense and it also changed the way in which EEC decision-making had been taking place. The supranational style of decision making (the Treaty of Rome had allowed for many Council decisions to be made by a large majority vote) was replaced by unanimity voting, which soon hampered European voting.

However, de Gaulle did not always get his own way. The French leader favored a stronger political union among the European states which would include foreign policy. At a summit in Bonn in 1961, the six Heads of State or Government investigated such a union at an intergovernmental committee chaired by French Ambassador Christian Fouchet. The Fouchet committee twice attempted to present the member states with a draft treaty that all member states could agree upon. No such agreement was reached, and it was not until 1969 that this issue was revisited.[58]

When the Treaty of Rome and the Euratom Treaty were agreed upon in 1957, they did not replace 1952's Treaty of Paris. This meant that the ECSC was still in existence alongside the EEC and Euratom. As stated in the Treaty of Rome, the ECSC shared the European Court of Justice and the Parliamentary Assembly with the EEC and Euratom, but the ECSC maintained its own executive. While the ECSC treaty gave strong supranational powers to the High Authority

---

[55] Moravcsik, "De Gaulle between Grain and *Grandeur* (Part 2)," 35.
[56] Moravcsik, "De Gaulle between Grain and *Grandeur* (Part 2)," 35.
[57] Moravcsik, "De Gaulle between Grain and *Grandeur* (Part 2)," 36.
[58] European Parliament, *The Historical Development of European Integration*, 7.

for the treaty's implementation, the Treaty of Rome and the Euratom Treaty were more like frameworks which made allowances for future legislation and gave more powers to the Council of Ministers.[59]

The question of uniting the three executives of the ECSC, the EEC, and Euratom was first mooted in 1958, but it was not until April 8, 1965, that the Merger Treaty was signed at an intergovernmental conference. The Common Agricultural Policy negotiations, Britain's attempt to join the EEC, and the "empty chair" crisis all caused delays to the merger of the three executives. The Merger Treaty, officially called The Treaty Establishing a Single Council and a Single Commission of the European Communities, finally entered into force on July 1, 1967. This treaty was significant because it marked the first time that a treaty had been reformed in the history of European integration.[60]

The new single Commission was more efficient and held increased political authority compared to its three separate predecessors. The European Parliamentary Assembly was also strengthened because it was now overseeing an executive with more powers and authority; the Assembly's decisions also carried more weight. Luxembourg had wanted compensation for the loss of the ECSC's High Authority. The European Court of Justice remained in Luxembourg, but the new consolidated Council made its home in Brussels, the city which increasingly became the "capital" of the European Communities and later the European Union.[61]

Prior to July 1, 1968, the European Commission (now calling itself "the Commission of the European Communities") declared that 18 months ahead of schedule, on that date, "the first and the major stage on the road to the economic unification of the European continent will be complete."[62] One of the aims of the Treaty of Rome, that of establishing a customs union, was to be realized. This meant that there would no longer be customs duties within the Common Market and all six member countries would adopt the same external customs tariff for export.[63] The EEC viewed this as a "decisive step in the economic history of the continent" – a significant step in unifying the European territory but by no means the final one.[64] With the adoption of the customs unions, the member countries were able to take advantage of economies of scale and businesses became more competitive in the global market. Trade increased, and with a then-population of 180 million people, the EEC became one of the largest economic powers in the world.[65]

---

[59] Finn Laursen, "The 1965 Merger Treaty: The First Reform of the Founding European Community Treaties," In Designing the European Union, edited by Finn Laursen, (London: Palgrave Macmillan, 2012), 77.

[60] Laursen, "The 1965 Merger Treaty," 78.

[61] Laursen, "The 1965 Merger Treaty," 94-95.

[62] "Declaration by the Commission of the European Communities (1 July 1968)," CVCE.eu, accessed March 30, 2020, https://www.cvce.eu/en/obj/declaration_by_the_commission_of_the_european_communities_1_july_1968-en-a4f5b96a-1d48-435b-9028-7e98739255d2.html

[63] To differentiate between tariffs and duties, tariffs are imposed on goods and duties are imposed on consumers.

[64] CVCE.eu, "Declaration by the Commission (1 July 1968)."

Expansion

When the Treaty of Rome was negotiated and signed, it had been with a view to future expansion of the EEC. After the UK first applied for membership in 1961 of what were then three Communities, Ireland, Denmark (also in 1961), and Norway (in 1962) were soon to follow.[66] However, the UK, Ireland, and Denmark did not become fully-fledged members of the EEC until January 1, 1973.[67]

1968 had been a tumultuous year in Europe. London, Paris, Berlin, and Rome had experienced mass political protests, but the USSR invasion of Czechoslovakia, student protests in Yugoslavia, and a political crisis in Poland also enveloped the continent. Hallstein's successor as President of the EEC Commission, the Belgian Jean Rey, publicly warned of a crisis threatening what the Community had thus far achieved. A European Parliament Congress met in The Hague on November 8-9, 1968, which demanded the rapid development of the EEC, including its expansion.[68] There is little doubt that the EEC perceived the "Prague Spring" in particular to be a threat, given that Soviet tanks had rolled into a territory that bordered West Germany.

Additionally, in November 1968 France underwent a currency crisis. The social unrest in France of six months earlier had resulted in a flight of capital from France to West Germany. The value of the French franc fell and the budget deficit soon grew. Fearful of the growth of West Germany's economy, not just the French but also the Americans and the British demanded that the deutschemark be allowed to appreciate.[69] West Germany was not willing to do this; nor was France, still led by de Gaulle for one more year, willing to allow the franc to be devalued. British ascension to the EEC was seen as a way to both strengthen the development of the EEC but also to prevent West German economic dominance.[70] When Georges Pompidou became President of France in 1969, he took a more favorable view than his predecessor de Gaulle had done regarding Britain's entry into the EEC. Pompidou also supported expanding the Common Market.[71]

---

[65] Donato Gómez-Díaz, "European Union," in *Encyclopedia of Business in Today's World*, ed. Charles Wankel (New York: Sage Publications, 2009): 626.

[66] Laursen, "The 1965 Merger Treaty," 78.

[67] In national referenda, Norway twice voted not to join the EEC or EU, in 1972 and in 1994. (Frank Emmert and Sinisa Petrovi, "The Past, Present, and Future of EU Enlargement," *Fordham International Law Journal* 37, no. 5 [2014]: 1352.)

[68] Loth, *Building Europe,* 162.

[69] Loth, *Building Europe,* 164.

[70] Loth, *Building Europe,* 165.

[71] Loth, *Building Europe,* 170.

Pompidou

The economies of Ireland and Denmark were closely tied to that of the UK, so when the UK began its negotiations to enter the EEC, parallel discussions were held with Ireland, Denmark and Norway, especially because all four countries were part of the EFTA.[72] The negotiations that took place in the early 1970s were undertaken in different conditions from the negotiations that had taken place in 1961 and 1967 (when de Gaulle once again vetoed Britain's entry to the EEC). The Common Market had been established and was in its final phase; common policies had shown to be working; and EEC legislation was more extensive than it had been in 1961, so it was clearer to the applicant countries which terms they would have to accept.[73]

During the negotiations the UK sought to change the economic terms desired by the EEC. The UK imported more of its agricultural products from non-EEC countries than the member

---

[72] "The United Kingdom's Accession to the EU," CVCE.eu, accessed April 7, 2020, https://www.cvce.eu/en/education/unit-content/-/unit/dd10d6bf-e14d-40b5-9ee6-37f978c87a01/3cf54bc7-03f0-4306-9f25-316d508d0c38

[73] CVCE.eu, "The United Kingdom's Accession to the EU."

countries, at lower prices. The Common Agricultural Policy was a particular sticking point. Nonetheless, throughout negotiations in 1971 a common ground was found. The UK accepted EEC preferences and agreed to contribute to the EEC budget that would gradually rise to 19% of the total EEC budget.[74] The six EEC member countries also held concerns about Britain's currency, the pound sterling. The pound was vulnerable to fluctuations in value due to high foreign credits and the British guarantee of Commonwealth countries' currency reserves, meaning that British economic policy was not in line with the Common Market nor any possible future currency union.[75] There was also a chronic deficit in the British balance of payments. The UK was importing more than it was exporting. Furthermore, there was also an imbalance between revenue and expenditure, and the UK held a large foreign debt.[76] In order to join the EEC the UK had to commit to a firmer economic stability policy. This was agreed in 1971, although the British would return to discuss their financial contribution to the EEC in the late 1980s.[77] In 1972, the UK, Ireland, and Denmark ratified the Treaty of Accession 1972 and became fully-fledged members of the EEC on January 1, 1973.[78]

Not until the 1970s did the issue of policing in the EEC reach the agenda. Although issues such as drug trafficking and money laundering had been discussed informally in the 1960s by the Pompidou Group, it took terrorist activities such as the hostage taking and attacks at the Munich Olympics of 1972 and further concerns about drug trafficking for an informal group to be convened. This group was founded at a European Council meeting in Rome on December 1, 1975. Some say the group was called the TREVI Group due to the proximity of its meeting place to the Trevi Fountain in Rome; others say TREVI is an acronym standing for *Terrorisme, Radicalisme, Extrémisme et Violence Internationale* in French.[79] Whatever its origin, the TREVI Group convened to ensure EEC cooperation in the fight against terrorism. This marked the first time in the history of the EEC that a proposal was put forward towards the idea about a European judicial area in criminal matters, and not just about the legal processes within the EEC itself. However, at this time the Netherlands vetoed this idea, preferring that such matters were left in charge of the Council of Europe.[80] Nonetheless, the creation of the TREVI group was important because it marked the first time that intra-European policing appeared on the agenda, and its aims were to come to more prominence when the Schengen Area came into being in the 1980s.[81]

---

[74] CVCE.eu, "The United Kingdom's Accession to the EU."
[75] Loth, *Building Europe,* 186.
[76] CVCE.eu, "The United Kingdom's Accession to the EU."
[77] CVCE.eu, "The United Kingdom's Accession to the EU."
[78] In 1974 and 1975 the UK further negotiated with the EEC. Britain's membership was not in question, but a European Regional Development fund was created which was largely beneficial to the UK. A correction mechanism for the country's budgetary contribution was also established. In June 1975, the British public voted in favor of remaining in the EEC by 67.2% (CVCE.eu, "The United Kingdom's Accession to the EU.")
[79] Alin Ciprian Gherman, "Cross-Border Police Cooperation in the European Union," *Annals of University of Oradea, Series: International Relations & European Studies* 7 (2015): 206.
[80] "Cross-Border Police Cooperation," Alin Ciprain Gherman, 206.
[81] When TREVI Group discussions were underway, INTERPOL, the International Criminal Police Organization was already in existence comprising several dozen countries, although INTERPOL did not become a Permanent

During the 1980s, the EEC member states started to discuss whether border checks between countries should be completely eliminated or if free movement should only apply to EEC nationals and not those of other nationalities traveling within the EEC.[82] The Benelux countries had already established a common passport area in 1970. Not all of the member states could agree on such an area, but given that France and West Germany had signed a bilateral agreement in 1984 allowing for freedom of movement between the two countries, on June 14, 1985, just five countries signed the Schengen Agreement in the town of Schengen, Luxembourg: Belgium, the Netherlands, Luxembourg, France and West Germany.[83] As part of the agreement, a single external border was established and passport checks were abolished. Visitors from outside the Schengen area were also allowed freedom of movement. However, the provisions of the agreement were not actually put into place until 1990, when the Schengen Convention was signed. Between 1985 and 1990, the Schengen area was more of an experiment to see if it would work and if it could successfully be rolled out to the rest of the EEC. Other countries joined the the Schengen area between 1990 and 1996: Italy, Portugal, Spain, Austria, Finland, Sweden, and Denmark.[84] Further countries joined as the EEC formally became the European Union and continued to expand. Non-EU members that were members of the EFTA (such as Switzerland, Norway, and Iceland) also joined the Schengen Area. The United Kingdom and Ireland never joined.

On January 1, 1986, the EEC grew from 10 members to 12 (Greece joined the Community on January 1, 1981). As had happened with the UK, Ireland and Denmark, the entry of Spain, Portugal, and Greece into the EEC was the result of several years of negotiations and fraught discussions. In order to become a member of the EEC, a country had to be a democracy. Spain returned to democracy on the death of General Franco in 1975. Portugal's dictatorship ended in 1974 and the first post-dictatorship democratic elections were held the following year. Greece returned to democracy in 1974 and applied for EEC membership the following year.[85] However, agricultural and budgetary issues delayed these three countries' entry to the EEC for several years. At the time, Spain's fishing fleet was larger than that of the entire EEC, which would have significantly affected fishing quotas. The climates of these three countries meant that vegetable, fruit, and olive oil could be imported into the northern countries more cheaply and earlier in the season, to the frustration of farmers in the northern countries. After years of negotiations Spain, Portugal, and Greece were allowed entry into the EEC, although Greece was given a five-year transition period in addition to restrictions of the free movement of workers and tomatoes until the end of 1987.[86] Spain was given a transition period of seven years on some products and ten

---

Observer of the United Nations until 1996 (Interpol.int, "Interpol and the United Nations," accessed April 7 2020, https://www.interpol.int/en/Our-partners/International-organization-partners/INTERPOL-and-the-United-Nations.

[82] Julia Gellatt, "Schengen and the Free Movement of People across Europe," Migrationpolicy.org, accessed April 9, 2020, https://www.migrationpolicy.org/article/schengen-and-free-movement-people-across-europe

[83] Gellatt, "Schengen and the Free Movement of People across Europe."

[84] Gellatt, "Schengen and the Free Movement of People across Europe."

[85] Emmert and Petrovi, "The Past, Present, and Future of EU Enlargement," 1366-1367.

years on other products before it was allowed full access to the internal market for its agricultural products.[87]

Much had occurred in the EEC between the mid-1970s and the formal ascension of Greece, Spain, and Portugal to the EEC. Problems arose between the Council and the European Parliament over ascension issues, because the Council (and member states) had originally held the power and control over EEC integration, but the Parliament had control over the EEC's ratification budget, and this control grew as the Community expanded.[88] A new framework was necessary to reflect the changing role of the European Parliament. In addition, three new leaders of the EEC's largest economies grew in power in the 1980s. French President François Mitterand was a socialist who was open to the possibility of a new treaty. Mitterand was opposed to any change to the Common Agricultural Policy, but he was willing to accept an expansion to the multinational powers of the EEC and greater collaboration between France and West Germany as this would strengthen France's position in Europe and indeed the world.[89] Helmut Kohl, the West German Chancellor, believed that Europe should operate as a federation and like Mitterand, he was open to a central role for West Germany and France.[90] British Prime Minister Margaret Thatcher favored less integration but more cooperation. She believed that the member states should hold the role as the center of European institutions and maintain strong decision making powers.[91]

---

[86] Emmert and Petrovi, "The Past, Present, and Future of EU Enlargement," 1370.
[87] Emmert and Petrovi, "The Past, Present, and Future of EU Enlargement," 1371.
[88] David Ramiro Troitiño, *European Integration: Building Europe*, (Hauppauge, New York: Nova Science Publishers, 2013): 97.
[89] Troitiño, *European Integration*, 99-100.
[90] Troitiño, *European Integration*, 100.
[91] Troitiño, *European Integration*, 100.

Mitterand

Thatcher

As a result of negotiations that started in the EEC in February 1986, the Single European Act of the 12 countries became effective on July 1, 1987. This Act was the first major revision to 1957´s Treaty of Rome, serving as a way to meet the needs of individual member states as well as integrate Europe more deeply in order to solve the problems that had arisen in the 1970s and 1980s. Particular focus was given to the creation of a single economic market, because the Common Market had not achieved the desired integration because there were still obstacles to trading inside the EEC.[92]

---

[92] Troitiño, *European Integration*, 101.

The Single European Act (SEA) provided for three principal provisions, namely the extension of the EEC's powers through a large internal market, an improvement to the decision-making powers of the Council of Ministers, and a growth in the role of European Parliament.[93] The SEA called for the creation of a fully operational internal market to be completed by January 1, 1993. This was to be a broadening of the common market objective introduced in 1957. New powers were established regarding monetary policy, social policy, economic and social cohesion, research and technological development, the environment, and cooperation in foreign policy.[94] With respect to the Council of Ministers, decision making was changed by introducing majority voting (instead of unanimity) in the existing areas of responsibility: amendment of the common customs tariff, the free movement of capital, the freedom to provide services, and the common sea and air transport policy. Furthermore, qualified majority voting was introduced to new areas: the internal market, social policy, economic and social cohesion, research and technological development, and environmental policy. This change to the way the Council voted was established as an amendment to the Council's internal rules of procedure.[95] The third major provision of the SEA addressed the strengthening of the European Parliament. With the adoption of the SEA, it was now enshrined in legislation that the assent of the European Parliament was required for EEC agreements on enlargement and association agreements. Moreover, a procedure for the Parliament's cooperation with the Council was introduced, which gave the Parliament greater legislative power than it had previously held.[96]

Looking East

Outside the EEC political events were unfolding in Central and Eastern Europe that would lead to great change to what would formally be called the European Union in 1992 under the Maastricht Treaty. In 1985, the General Secretary of the Soviet Union, Mikhail Gorbachev, introduced the policies of *perestroika* (economic reconstruction) and *glasnost* (increased political transparency).[97] The adoption of these policies meant that Gorbachev had to curb the USSR's international commitments as well as decrease its military expenditure as a way to slow down the economic and moral decline of the USSR.[98] The Soviet Union's economy had been stagnating when compared to the economies of the United States, Japan, and Western Europe, and it was plain to see that the current system was not working. The decline was moral too, because economic decisions were based on corrupt personal relationships, the distribution of goods and services was not equal, and shortages meant that theft and bribery were common. Gorbachev's reforms led to the disruption of centralized planning which was not replaced by any real market

---

[93] European Parliament, *The Historical Development of European Integration*, 9.
[94] European Parliament, *The Historical Development of European Integration*, 9.
[95] European Parliament, *The Historical Development of European Integration*, 9.
[96] European Parliament, *The Historical Development of European Integration*, 9.
[97] CVCE.eu, "The Eastern Bloc in the Throes of Change and the Implosion of the Soviet Bloc," accessed April 13, 2020, https://www.cvce.eu/en/education/unit-content/-/unit/1f5d29d1-bc79-44af-ae41-6fdb3f41608e/efe322ab-d857-4dd8-a835-a144be810893
[98] "The Eastern Block in the Throes of Change," CVCE.eu.

mechanisms.[99] Reduced production led to shortages and strikes. Discontent with Gorbachev's new policies could now be more openly expressed under *glasnost*. By the middle of 1991, several Soviet republics had declared their independence from the USSR in an attempt to implement national policies to save their economies and assert political autonomy. (The first three former republics to leave were Latvia, Estonia, and Lithuania in 1989, countries which would later to go on to join the European Union.) The Soviet Union ceased to exist on December 25, 1991. However, it was the fall of the Berlin Wall on November 9, 1989 that was a catalyst for non-USSR nations to reject Communism and move towards democracy and more market-based economies.

Gorbachev

Starting in 1988 and continuing into 1989, East Germans were calling for a liberalization of the East German regime. A "third way" was proposed by reformers – in order to avoid East Germany's absorption into West Germany, this "third way" would take elements from both Stalinist socialism and West Germany's liberal capitalism. However, the people of East Germany rejected this "third way." They wanted freedom of thought, freedom of the press, freedom of assembly, and the prosperity that West Germans enjoyed.[100] East Germans had started to escape

---

[99] "The Eastern Block in the Throes of Change," CVCE.eu.

to the West in 1989 due to more relaxed policies in Hungary, Czechoslovakia and Poland. The leader of the East German Government, Erich Honecker, expected Soviet support to help save the East German regime. However, Gorbachev, bearing in mind his rapprochement with the West, told Helmut Kohl in a visit to Bonn, Germany in June 1989 that the Soviet Union would not intervene militarily in East Germany.[101] Gorbachev tried to persuade Honecker to proceed with reforms along the lines of *perestroika*, but Honecker refused. Honecker was deposed in October 1989. The new leader of the Communist Party and the Head of Government did not adopt Honecker's rigid attitude, but this was not enough to placate the East German people. On November 4, 1989, a million East Berliners were protesting in the city's Alexanderplatz. Five days later, on November 9, the East Berlin authorities caved to the pressure and authorized travel abroad. Immediately, thousands of East Berliners crossed to West Berlin while demolishing portions of the Berlin Wall, and within days several million East Germans had visited West Berlin.[102] On November 10, the East German authorities announced that free and secret elections would take place within months. The Socialist reformers were defeated in these elections, and on April 12, 1990, the head of the GDR (East Germany) expressed his wish to see a unified Germany within NATO and the European Community.[103]

In Poland, economic strikes in 1988 led to widespread protests which led to trade union solidarity and semi-legal elections that led to the demise of the Communist Party. In May 1989, the "Iron Curtain" that separated Hungary from Austria had been dismantled, which allowed East Germans to flee to the West, and by the end of the year Hungary's Stalinist constitution had been abandoned. Czechoslovakia and Bulgaria soon adopted new constitutions in 1990 and 1991. Violent demonstrations in Romania led to the execution of the communist leader Nicolae Ceaușescu on December 25, 1991, while the fragmentation of Yugoslavia led to bloody civil wars.[104] After periods of transition, most of these countries later joined the European Union in one form or another - Czechoslovakia split into the Czech Republic and Slovakia, and to date, Slovenia and Croatia are the only former Yugoslav republics to join the European Union.

The unification of Germany increased the size of Germany in the Community, although there were few changes to EEC institutions. The size of German representation increased and the region of the former East Germany received EEC economic aid, although this was similar to aid that Italy, Spain, Greece, Portugal, and Ireland had previously received.[105] The EEC also

---

[100] CVCE.eu, "The Collapse of the GDR and the Fall of the Berlin Wall," accessed April 13, 2020, https://www.cvce.eu/en/education/unit-content/-/unit/1f5d29d1-bc79-44af-ae41-6fdb3f41608e/d236de7f-d57a-4054-9c9a-1f977b5a3db5
[101] CVCE.eu, "The Collapse of the GDR and the Fall of the Berlin Wall."
[102] CVCE.eu, "The Collapse of the GDR and the Fall of the Berlin Wall."
[103] CVCE.eu, "The Collapse of the GDR and the Fall of the Berlin Wall."
[104] "The Collapse of Communist Regimes in Eastern Europe," CVCE.eu, accessed April 13, 2020, https://www.cvce.eu/en/education/unit-content/-/unit/1f5d29d1-bc79-44af-ae41-6fdb3f41608e/de5ef049-acec-4e19-983c-27104320cd2b.
[105] "The European Community and East Germany," CVCE.eu, accessed April 14, 2020, https://www.cvce.eu/en/education/unit-content/-/unit/1f5d29d1-bc79-44af-ae41-6fdb3f41608e/03167992-d38d-

extended financial aid for economic restructuring and private investment to former Communist countries that would later become EU members. Between 1991 and 1996 the EEC/EU established Association Agreements with Poland, Hungary, Romania, Bulgaria, the Czech Republic, Slovakia, Estonia, Latvia, Lithuania, and Slovenia. These agreements were contingent upon progress being made with regard to human rights, multiparty democracy, and economic liberalization.[106] The purpose of these agreements was to prepare these countries to eventual ascension to the European Union.

The Creation of the European Union

The fall of communist regimes in Central and Eastern Europe led to the Maastricht Treaty, also known as the Treaty on the European Union, being signed on February 7, 1992, and the Treaty came into force on November 1, 1993. "By instituting a European Union, the Maastricht Treaty marked a new step in the process of creating an 'ever-closer union among the peoples of Europe.'"[107] The Maastricht Treaty contained provisions for the new countries that were expected to join in due course. This European Union had a single institutional structure, comprising the Council, the European Parliament, the European Commission, the Court of Justice, and the Court of Auditors (the Court of Auditors had originally been established in 1975 to provide financial oversight). Two further bodies were established: the Economic and Social Committee and a Committee of the Regions. Both of these committees held advisory powers. While the European Investment Bank and the European Investment Fund were already operation, a European System of Central Banks and an overall European Central Bank were newly created.[108] The European System of Central Banks was a consortium of the European Central Bank and the national banks of each member state designed to coordinate financial policies although each member state maintained its independence; the European Central Bank was established to prepare the ground for the European common currency.[109] Only member states of the common currency – the euro, which came into circulation in 2002 – were members of the European Central Bank.

The Treaty of Maastricht created three essential "pillars" of the European Union. The first "pillar" was made up of the European Communities (the European Economic Community, the European Coal and Steel Community, and the European Atomic Energy Commission), and a framework was provided within which the Community institutions could exercise the powers that member states had transferred to the new European Union according to the new Treaty. The European Union's task was "to make the single market work and to promote, among other

---

4f75-90f7-a8b69492bda3

[106] "European Community and Aid to Eastern Europe." CVCE.eu. Accessed April 14, 2020. https://www.cvce.eu/en/education/unit-content/-/unit/1f5d29d1-bc79-44af-ae41-6fdb3f41608e/d41c0d3f-3bed-4585-a9a9-1a13320f39b9

[107] European Parliament, *The Historical Development of European Integration*, 10.

[108] European Parliament, *The Historical Development of European Integration*, 10.

[109] Loth, *Building Europe,* 331.

things, a harmonious, balanced and sustainable development of economic activities, a high level of employment and of social protection and equality between men and women."[110] The Common Market was established and the single monetary policy was initiated.

The second "pillar" was the Common Foreign and Security Policy (CFSP). Using intergovernmental methods, the Union defined and implemented the CFSP: "The [m]ember [s]tates were to support this policy actively and unreservedly in a spirit of loyalty and mutual solidarity. Its objectives were: to safeguard the common values, fundamental interests, independence and integrity of the Union in conformity with the principles of the United Nations Charter; to strengthen the security of the Union in all ways; to promote international cooperation; to develop and consolidate democracy and the rule of law, and respect for human rights and fundamental freedoms."[111]

The final "pillar" of the European Union was cooperation in the fields of justice and home affairs. This "pillar" covered the rules and controls regarding: crossing the EU's external borders; combating terrorism, serious crime, drug trafficking, and international fraud; the creation of a European Police Force (Europol) so that information could be exchanged between national police forces more easily; judicial cooperation in both criminal and civil matters; controls on illegal immigration; and a common policy for asylum seekers.[112] In short, the objective of the third "pillar" was to provide EU citizens with a high level of safety in spheres including freedom, security, and justice.

While the Maastricht Treaty came about with a view to enlarge the Union with the membership of former Communist countries, the next enlargement on January 1, 1995, featured three countries that did not have to transition from Communist to democratic rule: Austria, Finland, and Sweden. All three countries had been members of the European Free Trade Agreement, but with the creation of the European Union, which had been a part of the European Economic Area Agreement with the EFTA countries, EFTA countries that were outside the EU held most of the rights to the EU and met almost all of the obligations of full EU membership, but they were excluded from participation in the EU institutions and their decision making.[113] The Swiss electorate rejected membership of European Economic Area Agreement. This agreement particularly suited Switzerland's neutrality, and without Swiss membership the European Economic Area Agreement lost some of its appeal to other states. The creation of the Common Foreign and Security Policy in the Maastricht Treaty was flexible enough to make EU membership palatable to other more neutral states. In the cases of Austria and Finland, the fall of the "Iron Curtain" ended restrictions on the international relations of these two countries.[114] After another Ascension Treaty in 1994, Austria, Finland, Sweden, and Norway applied to be full

---

[110] European Parliament, *The Historical Development of European Integration*, 10.
[111] European Parliament, *The Historical Development of European Integration*, 11.
[112] European Parliament, *The Historical Development of European Integration*, 11.
[113] Emmert and Petrovi, "The Past, Present, and Future of EU Enlargement," 1371.
[114] Emmert and Petrovi, "The Past, Present, and Future of EU Enlargement," 1372.

members of the European Union. For the second time, Norwegian voters rejected EU membership in a national referendum (the first time being in 1972), so the addition of Austria, Finland, and Sweden increased European Union membership to 15 member states.[115]

The European Union was further strengthened by the Treaty of Amsterdam, signed on October 2, 1997, and effected on May 1, 1999. The Treaty of Amsterdam saw several amendments to the Maastricht Treaty on European Union and the Treaties Establishing European Communities, although much of the legislation bolstered what was in the Maastricht Treaty rather than creating any new institutions or establishing new objectives. Social policy, largely covered by the third "pillar" of the Maastricht Treaty was further strengthened, and greater cooperation within the Schengen Area was agreed upon. Within the European Union, intergovernmental police and judicial collaboration was enhanced. With the exception of agricultural and competition policies, the European Parliament was now on an equal footing with the Council in terms of being co-legislators. The Parliament also gained the power to approve the person chosen as the future President of the Commission. The Amsterdam Treaty also removed from the European Treaties any provisions which had become obsolete. Further provisions were made for the addition of new member states to the European Union, a planned number which in 1999 stood at 20.[116]

Prior to the fall of the communist governments and the ratification of the Maastricht Treaty, the idea of Economic and Monetary Union (EMU) was first mooted in 1988 under a committee chaired by the Frenchman Jacques Delors, then President of the European Commission. The first stage of the Economic and Monetary Union was to begin on July 1, 1990, a date on which all restrictions on the movement of capital within the EEC were to be abolished. Further negotiations were agreed in December 1991 and were signed as part of the Maastricht Treaty in February 1992, although the Protocol on the Statute of the European System of Central Banks and of the European Central Bank did not come into being until November 1, 1993.[117]

---

[115] The 12 stars featured on the European Union flag have never had anything to do with the twelve member states that comprised the EEC as of 1986. The 12 yellow stars on a blue background had been the symbol of the European Council dating back to the days of the six-member European Coal and Steel Community in 1955.

[116] European Parliament, *The Historical Development of European Integration*, 11-13.

[117] Ecb.europa.eu, "Economic and Monetary Union (EMU)," accessed April 14, 2020, https://www.ecb.europa.eu/ecb/history/emu/html/index.en.html

Delors

The second stage of the EMU started with the establishment of the Economic Monetary Institute (EMI) on January 1, 1994. At this stage the EMI had no real power to drive monetary policy or to intervene in exchange rates in the European Union, but the EMI was tasked with strengthening central bank cooperation, coordinating monetary policy, making preparations for the establishment of the European System of Central Banks, and the eventual creation of the single currency.[118] The European Council decided that the new currency would be called the "euro" at the end of December 1995 and a new exchange rate mechanism was established the following year. In 1998, 11 member states were deemed ready to join the euro: Belgium, Germany, Spain, France, Ireland, Italy, Luxembourg, the Netherlands, Austria, Portugal, and Finland. On January 1, 1999, the third and final stage of the EMU began with a fixing of the

---

[118] "Economic and Monetary Union (EMU)," Ecb.europa.eu.

exchange rates of the 11 member state currencies, with all agreeing to the single monetary policy under the responsibility of the European Central Bank.[119] On January 1, 2002, euro banknotes and coins went into general circulation.

While the Treaty of Amsterdam had made several amendments to the Maastricht Treaty and former treaties with more of a view to strengthen the European Union, the Treaty of Nice (signed in February 2001 and made effective on February 1, 2003) made amendments to the previous two treaties with a greater focus on the impending eastward expansion. (The European Coal and Steel Community ceased to exist in 2002, with all of its activities absorbed by the Treaties of Amsterdam and Nice). Adjustments were made to the composition and powers of the various institutions: The Council, The Commission, the European Parliament, and the Court of Justice being the principal institutions, to prepare the European Union for its largest expansion seen to date. Provisions were also made for enhanced cooperation and the protection of fundamental rights.[120] Overnight, on January 1, 2004, the 15 members of the European Union became 25. The former Communist countries – the Czech Republic, Estonia, Hungary, Latvia, Lithuania, Poland, Slovakia, and Slovenia – were added to the Union, as were Cyprus and Malta.

The last major Treaty ratified in the European Union was the Treaty of Lisbon, signed by member states in 2007 and made effective on December 1, 2009 (Bulgaria and Romania joined the Union on January 1, 2007). The Treaty of Lisbon amended both the Treaty of the European Union (Treaty of Maastricht) and the Treaty establishing the European Community. Henceforth, the word "Community" was replaced by the word "Union" throughout the text.[121] The Union officially became the legal successor to the European Community. The Treaty of Lisbon did not grant the European Union any new powers, but it amended the way existing powers were exercised. There was a further enhancement to citizen participation and protection as well as a modification to decision-making processes to increase efficiency and transparency. The aim of the Treaty was to increase parliamentary scrutiny and democratic accountability.[122]

The Lisbon Treaty clarified some of the powers of the Union for the first time. It distinguishes between four types of competences: exclusive competence, where the Union alone can legislate, and Member States only implement; shared competence, where the Member States can legislate and adopt legally binding measures if the Union has not already done so; and supporting competence, where the EU adopts measures to support or complement Member States' policies. Union competences can also now be handed back to the Member States in the course of a treaty revision. The Treaty of Lisbon also established the European Union as a legal entity able to sign international treaties or join an international organization. Member states can only sign

---

[119] "Economic and Monetary Union (EMU)," Ecb.europa.eu. The number of member countries of the Euro eventually grew to 19 countries: Greece joined in 2001, followed by Slovenia in 2007, Cyprus and Malta in 2008, Slovakia in 2009, Estonia in 2011, Latvia in 2014, and Lithuania in 2015.

[120] European Parliament, *The Historical Development of European Integration*, 14-16.

[121] European Parliament, *The Historical Development of European Integration*, 18.

[122] European Parliament, *The Historical Development of European Integration*, 18.

international agreements that are compatible with EU law.[123]

"Third" pillar aspects from the Treaty of Maastricht were fully absorbed into "first" pillar aspects in the Treaty of Lisbon, i.e. freedom, security, and justice are no longer separate from the European institutions that implement or ensure them. Another change was that the European Parliament is now able to propose amendments to the Treaties, which was a power that was previously held by the Council, a member state government or the Commission. Although the European Convention on Human Rights did not come into force until June 1, 2010, the Charter of Fundamental Rights is included in one of the articles of the Lisbon Treaty. It is also quite notable that for the first time in the history of European integration a procedure was established under Article 50 of the Treaty of Lisbon which provided for any member state to withdraw from the Union in accordance with its national constitutional requirements.[124]

In the last decade, the European Union has faced two major crises and the secession of one of its larger member states. On a positive note, the EU was honored with the Nobel Peace Prize in 2012 for "over six decades contributed to the advancement of peace and reconciliation, democracy and human rights in Europe."[125] Croatia also became the 28th member of the European Union on July 1, 2013. However, the Eurozone debt crisis, the migrant crisis, and departure of the United Kingdom from the European overshadowed some of the Union's more positive achievements.

The Eurozone crisis did not badly affect countries like Germany, France, or the Netherlands; while countries such as Ireland, Portugal, Spain, Greece were the worst affected. The Eurozone crisis was triggered by the global economic recession of 2008, when cross-border capital inflows stopped.[126] The countries with high debt-to-GDP ratios were not the worst hit; instead, those with current account deficits, or who had heavily relied on foreign lending, suffered the most.[127] Greece (twice), Ireland, Spain, Portugal, and Cyprus required bailouts from either the European Central Bank and/or the International Monetary Fund. Unemployment rates in Spain and Greece reached 27%. In the 1980s and 1990s, it was believed that financial integration (introduced before the common currency) would lead to both convergence and macroeconomic stability.[128] However, this most certainly did not occur. The economies of countries on the "periphery" of the EU proved to be more vulnerable than countries like France and Germany in the "center." The Eurozone crisis showed that a "one-size-fits-all" economic policy does not work well in the

---

[123] European Parliament, *The Historical Development of European Integration*, 19.
[124] European Parliament, *The Historical Development of European Integration*, 19.
[125] "The Nobel Peace Prize 2012," Nobelprize.org, Accessed April 14, 2020, https://www.nobelprize.org/prizes/peace/2012/summary/

[126] Richard Baldwin and Francesco Giavazzi, "Introduction," In The Eurozone Crisis: A Consensus View of the Crisis and a Few Possible Solutions, edited by Richard Baldwin and Francesco Giavazzi, (London: Centre for Economic Research, 2015): 19.
[127] Baldwin and Giavazzi, "Introduction," 20.
[128] Baldwin and Giavazzi, "Introduction," 56.

Eurozone when a global recession occurs, and the European Union will have to change its economic and financial policies in order to avoid such a crisis occurring again.

The migrant crisis hit the EU particularly hard in 2015 and 2016. Over one million migrants and refugees reached European shores, many of them coming from war-torn Syria. The European Union has some of the highest common asylum standards in the world, but the rules that apply to asylum seekers and refugees do not apply to economic migrants whose lives are not in danger. Many of the migrants and refugees who arrived in the EU reached its southern shores, i.e. Greece, Italy, or neighboring Turkey, and then proceeded to take advantage of the open borders of the Schengen area to reach countries further north such as Germany, Sweden, and the UK.[129] Legitimate asylum seekers and refugees are expected to seek shelter in the first safe country that they come to. Greece and Italy (and Turkey) were overwhelmed by the number of people who arrived on their shores. The aid that the European Union was expected to offer was made more difficult by the humanitarian outcry at the thousands of people who tried to arrive but lost their lives in the attempt do so and the inability to determine whether recent arrivals were refugees or economic migrants. EU member states agreed to a voluntary resettlement program, which saw migrants and refugees settled in 21 member states. However, such was the emergency that in 2016 a European Border and Coast Guard was established to protect the EU's common external borders.[130] Countries in Central and Eastern Europe were generally less willing to admit refugees and asylum seekers than countries in northern Europe. The numbers of people seeking to arrive in Europe in 2018 and 2019 were much reduced when compared to the previous three years, but the European Union will have to devise a realistic policy to distinguish genuine asylum seekers and refugees from economic migrants and ensure that the EU has the means to accept such large numbers of arrivals should another refugee/migrant crisis occur.

The Treaty of Lisbon had established Article 50, the procedure by which a member state could elect to leave the European Union. It was invoked by the United Kingdom in 2016, after a referendum vote of 51.9% in favor of leaving the Union and 48.1% against. The Prime Minister, David Cameron, resigned as a result of the vote.[131] The UK had never had an entirely easy relationship with the EU. It had declined to join the ECSC because it also shared strong economic ties with the United States and the Commonwealth. Charles de Gaulle vetoed Britain's application to join the EEC twice. Although Margaret Thatcher was an early protagonist of the Single Market and neoliberal policies within the EU, she was more antagonistic towards monetary union and a shared social policy.[132] The UK left the Exchange-Rate Mechanism in September 1992 and never joined the euro. The United Kingdom Independence Party (UKIP) became a growing voice of popular if not electoral dissent against Europe in the 21st century, in

---

[129] European Commission, "The EU and the Migrant Crisis." Brussels: European Union, 2017.

[130] European Commission, "The EU and the Migrant Crisis."

[131] Simon Bulmer and Lucia Quaglia, "The Politics and Economics of Brexit," *Journal of European Economic Policy* 25 no. 8 (2018): 1089.

[132] Bulmer and Quaglia, "The Politics and Economics of Brexit," 1091.

addition to a growing number of Euro-sceptics in David Cameron's own Conservative Party. In a speech in 2015, Cameron set out his vision for the UK, in which he wanted a new settlement with the EU and he promised the British public a referendum. The European Council agreement was reached in February 2016, but the Conservative Party were divided during the referendum campaign and the leader of the opposition Labour Party, Jeremy Corbyn, showed little enthusiasm for campaigning in favour of the UK remaining in the EU.[133] In March 2017, under Conservative Prime Minister Theresa May, the UK invoked Article 50 of the Lisbon Treaty. A leaving date of March 31, 2019, was delayed until October 31, 2019, which was delayed again until the UK finally left the EU on January 31, 2020. In early 2020, the UK was still undergoing a transition period before it fully leaves.

The European Union, which started from the desire of western European countries to never suffer the horrors of the First and Second World Wars again and to unite due to shared cultural, political, and economic ideals, became a small community of six member states in the European Coal and Steel Community, and later grew into a political and economic union which featured 28 countries and more than 500 million people prior to the UK's departure. Other parts of the world have created military alliances and economic trading blocks, but none on the scale of the European Union.

The study of how the European Union came to be until the present moment is a study of the evolution of a political, social, and economic union in which member states were (largely) able to overcome their differences, expand according to well established treaties and stable institutions able to absorb new members, adjust according to political developments and the fall of Communism on the eastern half of the continent, and survive economic turmoil and a refugee crisis of an estimated one million arrivals, many of whom did not share the cultural values or political ideals of the European Union. The growth of the EU demonstrates how countries from different parts of Europe were able to find common ground and agree to different policies without sacrificing their national identities.

The future of the European Union cannot be certain. Another economic recession (possibly provoked by COVID-19) will test the strength of the EU's Common Market and the Eurozone. Turkey has attempted to join the European Union, but cultural concerns (the EU has no majority-Muslim member state), unease about Turkey's human rights record, and questions about Turkey's commitment to democracy make it unlikely that the current 27 EU states will unanimously agree to accept Turkey into the EU. As was the case with the UK, other European member states may choose to leave the Union one day. However, it cannot be doubted that since the creation of the Economic Coal and Steel Community and as the political and economic union expanded eastwards, peace has reigned in Europe like never before in European history. The European Union is currently the world's second biggest economy and its citizens enjoy a freedom of movement that no one else on Earth does. The EU also upholds high human rights

---

133 Bulmer and Quaglia, "The Politics and Economics of Brexit," 1092.

standards, and upholding these standards is a requisite of membership. While it cannot be said that the European Union has established a utopian confederation, it has been successful in achieving most of the objectives it has set out to accomplish.

Online Resources

Other 20th century titles by Charles River Editors

Other titles about the European Union on Amazon

Further Reading

"About the Council of Europe – Overview." Council of Europe. Accessed March 26, 2020. https://www.coe.int/en/web/yerevan/the-coe/about-coe/overview.

Baldwin, Richard and Francesco Giavazzi. "Introduction." In The Eurozone Crisis: A Consensus View of the Crisis and a Few Possible Solutions, edited by Richard Baldwin and Francesco Giavazzi, 18-60. London: Centre for Economic Research, 2015.

Baylis, John. "Britain and the Dunkirk Treaty: The Origins of NATO." *Journal of Strategic Studies* 5 no. 2 (1982): 236-247.

The Brussels Treaty, Mar. 17, 1948, AE TC 365, Aug. 25, 1948.

Bulmer, Simon and Lucia Quaglia. "The Politics and Economics of Brexit." *Journal of European Economic Policy* 25 no. 8 (2018): 1089-1098.

Churchill, Winston. "Winston Churchill's Speech." Speech, University of Zurich, Zurich, September 19, 1946.

"The Collapse of Communist Regimes in Eastern Europe." CVCE.eu. Accessed April 13, 2020. https://www.cvce.eu/en/education/unit-content/-/unit/1f5d29d1-bc79-44af-ae41-6fdb3f41608e/de5ef049-acec-4e19-983c-27104320cd2b.

"The Collapse of the GDR and the Fall of the Berlin Wall." CVCE.eu. Accessed April 13, 2020. https://www.cvce.eu/en/education/unit-content/-/unit/1f5d29d1-bc79-44af-ae41-6fdb3f41608e/d236de7f-d57a-4054-9c9a-1f977b5a3db5.

"Declaration by the Commission of the European Communities (1 July 1968)." CVCE.eu. Accessed March 30, 2020. https://www.cvce.eu/en/obj/declaration_by_the_commission_of_the_european_communities_1_july_1968-en-a4f5b96a-1d48-435b-9028-7e98739255d2.html.

"The Eastern Bloc in the Throes of Change and the Implosion of the Soviet Bloc." CVCE.eu.

Accessed April 13, 2020. https://www.cvce.eu/en/education/unit-content/-/unit/1f5d29d1-bc79-44af-ae41-6fdb3f41608e/efe322ab-d857-4dd8-a835-a144be810893.

"Economic and Monetary Union (EMU)." Ecb.europa.eu. Accessed April 14, 2020. https://www.ecb.europa.eu/ecb/history/emu/html/index.en.html.

"The EEC Institutions." CVCE.eu. Accessed March 27, 2020. https://www.cvce.eu/en/education/unit-content/-/unit/1c8aa583-8ec5-41c4-9ad8-73674ea7f4a7/bd64db50-fa41-4fb1-b3bd-4f99d2cfee2d.

Emmert, Frank and Sinisa Petrovi. "The Past, Present, and Future of EU Enlargement." *Fordham International Law Journal* 37 no. 5 (2014): 1349-1420.

European Commission. *The EU and the Migrant Crisis*. Brussels: European Union, 2017.

"European Community and Aid to Eastern Europe." CVCE.eu. Accessed April 14, 2020. https://www.cvce.eu/en/education/unit-content/-/unit/1f5d29d1-bc79-44af-ae41-6fdb3f41608e/d41c0d3f-3bed-4585-a9a9-1a13320f39b9.

"The European Community and East Germany." CVCE.eu. Accessed April 14, 2020. https://www.cvce.eu/en/education/unit-content/-/unit/1f5d29d1-bc79-44af-ae41-6fdb3f41608e/03167992-d38d-4f75-90f7-a8b69492bda3.

European Parliament. *The Historical Development of European Integration*. Brussels: European Parliament, 2018.

Gellatt, Julia. "Schengen and the Free Movement of People across Europe." Migrationpolicy.org. Accessed April 9, 2020. https://www.migrationpolicy.org/article/schengen-and-free-movement-people-across-europe.

Gherman, Alin Ciprian. "Cross-Border Police Cooperation in the European Union." *Annals of University of Oradea, Series: International Relations & European Studies 7 (*2015): 203-216.

Gómez-Díaz, Donato. "European Union." In *Enciclopedia of Business in Today's World*, edited by Charles Wankel, 623-628. New York: Sage Publication, 2009.

"Interpol and the United Nations." Interpol.int. Accessed April 7, 2020. https://www.interpol.int/en/Our-partners/International-organization-partners/INTERPOL-and-the-United-Nations.

Laurent, Pierre-Henri. "Paul-Henri Spaak and the Diplomatic Origins of the Common Market, 1955-1956." *Political Science Quarterly* 85 no. 3 (1970): 373-396.

Laursen, Finn. "The 1965 Merger Treaty: The First Reform of the Founding European

Community Treaties." In *Designing the European Union*, edited by Finn Laursen, 77-97. London: Palgrave Macmillan, 2012.

Lehmann, Wilhelm and Christian, Salm. *Walter Hallstein: First President of the Commission and Visionary of European Integration*, Research Report prepared for the European Parliamentary Research Service. Luxembourg: European Parliament, 2019.

Loth, Wilfred. *Building Europe: A History of European Unification*. Berlin: De Gruyter Oldenbourg, 2015.

Mathieu, Gilbert. "The History of the ECSC: Good Times and Bad," *Le Monde*, May 9, 1970, https://www.cvce.eu/en/obj/the_history_of_the_ecsc_good_times_and_bad_from_le_monde_9_may_1970-en-54f09b32-1b0c-4060-afb3-5e475dcafda8.html.

Moravcsik, Andrew. "De Gaulle Between Grain and *Grandeur*: The Political Economy of French EC Policy," 1958–1970 (Part 1)." *Journal of Cold War Studies* 2 no. 2, (2000): 3–43.

Moravcsik, Andrew. "De Gaulle Between Grain and *Grandeur*: The Political Economy of French EC Policy," 1958–1970 (Part 2)." *Journal of Cold War Studies* 2 no. 3, (2000): 4–68.

"The Nobel Peace Prize 2012." Nobelprize.org. Accessed April 14, 2020. https://www.nobelprize.org/prizes/peace/2012/summary/

"Organisation for European Economic Co-operation." OECD. Accessed March 26, 2020. http://www.oecd.org/general/organisationforeuropeaneconomicco-operation.htm.

Treaty Establishing the European Coal and Steel Community, April 18, 1951, auteur: x, July 23, 1952.

Treaty Establishing the European Economic Community, March 25, 1957, [s.d. 378 p], January 1, 1958.

Troitiño, David Ramiro. *European Integration: Building Europe*. Hauppauge, New York: Nova Science Publishers, 2013.

"The United Kingdom's Accession to the EU." CVCE.eu. Accessed April 7, 2020. https://www.cvce.eu/en/education/unit-content/-/unit/dd10d6bf-e14d-40b5-9ee6-37f978c87a01/3cf54bc7-03f0-4306-9f25-316d508d0c38.

Vanke, Jeffrey. "The Treaty of Rome and Europeanism." *The Journal of the Historical Society* 7 no. 4 (2007): 443-474.

Free Books by Charles River Editors

We have brand new titles available for free most days of the week. To see which of our titles are currently free, click on this link.

Discounted Books by Charles River Editors

We have titles at a discount price of just 99 cents everyday. To see which of our titles are currently 99 cents, click on this link.

www.ingramcontent.com/pod-product-compliance
Lightning Source LLC
Chambersburg PA
CBHW081400160726
48000CB00010B/3430